Christmas 1991

To G... ...m
Viv... off
...zie.
α.

D0432426

1 9 8 3
The Year
I Was Born

Compiled by Sally Tagholm

Illustrated by Michael Evans

FANTAIL

in association with Signpost Books

FANTAIL PUBLISHING, AN IMPRINT OF PUFFIN ENTERPRISES
Published by the Penguin Group
Penguin Books Ltd, 27 Wrights Lane, London W8 5TZ, England
Penguin Books USA Inc., 375 Hudson Street, New York, NY 10014, USA
Penguin Books Australia Ltd., Ringwood, Victoria, Australia
Penguin Books Canada Ltd, 10 Alcorn Avenue, Toronto, Ontario, Canada
M4V 3B2
Penguin Books (NZ) Ltd, 182–190 Wairau Road, Auckland 10, New Zealand

Penguin Books Ltd., Registered Offices: Harmondsworth, Middlesex,
England

First published 1990
Published by Penguin Books in association with Signpost Books
10 9 8 7 6

Based on an original idea by Sally Wood
Conceived, designed and produced by Signpost Books Ltd, 1989
Copyright in this format © 1990 Signpost Books Ltd.,
25 Eden Drive, Headington, Oxford OX3 0AB, England

Illustrations copyright © 1990 Michael Evans
Text copyright © 1990 Sally Tagholm

Paste-up: Naomi Games
Editor: Dorothy Wood

ISBN 0140 90201 5

All rights reserved

Colour separations by Fotographics, Ltd.
Printed and bound in Belgium by Proost Book Production through
Landmark Production Consultants, Ltd.

Typeset by AKM Associates (UK) Ltd, Ajmal House, Hayes Road,
Southall, London

All rights reserved. Without limiting the rights under copyright reserved
above, no part of this publication may be reproduced, stored in or
introduced into a retrieval system, or transmitted, in any form or by any
means (electronic, mechanical, photocopying, recording or otherwise),
without the prior written permission of both the copyright owner and
the above publisher of this book.

ME

Name: Gail.R.Poole
Date of birth: 24th November
Time of birth:
Place of birth: S.t.Georges (London)
Weight at birth:
Colour of eyes: Lt. Brown
Colour of hair (if any): Goldy browny
Distinguishing marks:

Mum

Dad

Sister/Brother

I'm an Only Child

Sister/Brother

MY FAMILY

January

Saturday
January 1

A chain of beacons is lit around the country to mark the beginning of the Boys' Brigade Centenary Year: the first at Leeds Castle in Kent.

Sunday
January 2

British ships and planes are on full alert for Danish trawlers fishing for sprats within a 19km zone of Newcastle.

Monday
January 3

Head of the GLC Ken Livingstone unveils a bronze statue of a woman holding a dove of peace in Jubilee Gardens, London, to mark the beginning of the Greater London Council's Peace Year.

Tuesday
January 4

Three people have been treated in hospital in Cambridgeshire after being hit by lids from exploding tins of treacle.

Wednesday
January 5

Trawlers help a Dutch coaster into Plymouth Sound after it is nearly driven onto the rocks in high seas and strong winds.

Thursday
January 6

Descendants of Alexander Selkirk, the real Robinson Crusoe, set off to put a plaque on the island where he was marooned in 1704.

Robinson Crusoe's Island

Friday
January 7

A solar-powered car crosses Australia from Perth to Sydney (4022 kms) in less than 20 days: average speed just under 29 mph.

Strong earthquakes in central California

Saturday
January 8

Mrs Thatcher arrives in the Falkland Islands after a secret 23-hour flight from Brize Norton in Oxfordshire.

Sunday
January 9

A load weighing 330 tonnes successfully negotiates an M1 bridge at Rotherham, which has been specially strengthened with super glue!

Monday
January 10

There is very little snow in the Swiss Alps and ski-ing is impossible below 1800m.

Tuesday
January 11

Happy third birthday to the Giannini sextuplets (4 boys and 2 girls) who live in Italy!

Wednesday
January 12

Cars are trapped by hundreds of litres of glue spilled by a lorry in High Road, Tottenham, London. Firemen spend 2 hours washing the road with detergent!

Thursday
January 13

A Sea King helicopter from *HMS Invincible* helps to rescue the crew of a Greek cargo ship in Force 9 gales in the English Channel.

Friday
January 14

Rose McGrory, from Ballynahinch, Northern Ireland, is crowned Miss Great Britain.

New Moon

January

Named after the Roman god Janus, who had two faces and could look backwards and forwards at the same time. Also known as 'frosty-month,' 'after-yule', 'first month' and 'snow-month'.

Boys' Brigade Year begins with bonfires and goes on with lots of special celebrations throughout the year. There are camps all over the world, thanksgiving services and a train (locomotive 86243) is named The Boys' Brigade in Glasgow! The Girls' Brigade started 10 years later in 1893.

January 26: The Post office issues four new stamps – British River Fishes

The Billingsgate Excavation

Last chance to see an important excavation at Billingsgate in London this month! Archeologists have been working for a year on the site by the river and have found the remains of medieval buildings, scabbards, a Saxon boot (whole), 17th century glass bottles, an 18th century fan, buckles and brooches!

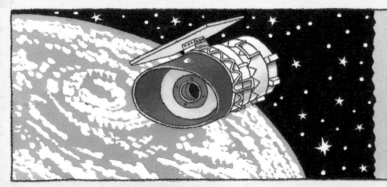

January 26: The Space Telescope

The space telescope is 3.6 metres long, weighs one tonne and cost £50 million. It is the first to orbit earth and will send back data to the tracking station in Oxfordshire. It will detect hidden, unknown stars by the tiny amount of heat they give off.

Saturday *January 15*	Demonstration in Caernarfon by the Welsh Language Society: they want Welsh learner drivers to carry 'D' rather than 'L' plates. 'Dysgwr' is Welsh for learner.
Sunday *January 16*	A White-Winged Crossbill, which usually lives in Scandinavia, is spotted on the banks of the river Derwent in Derbyshire.
Monday *January 17*	BBC Breakfast Time starts 6.30am. Earthquakes in Greece and southern Italy.
Tuesday *January 18*	David Bellamy, who is protesting about a proposed new dam in Tasmania, spends his 50th birthday in Risdon Jail, near Hobart.

The Kilauea volcano in Hawaii erupts

Wednesday *January 19*	Ham, the first American chimpanzee in space, has died in a North Carolina Zoo, aged 26.
Thursday *January 20*	Mini Flu Alert! A minor form of flu, called respiratory syncytial virus infection, is sweeping the country.
Friday *January 21*	The last of 8 chimneys over 90m high is blown up at the British Steel works at Corby, Northamptonshire, which closed 2 years ago.
Saturday *January 22*	Vesna, a German Shepherd dog, has crossed the whole of Russia (more than 1770km) to find her master. She set off in April 1979.

Earthquake in northern Italy

Sunday *January 23*	The 4-tonne Soviet satellite Cosmos-1402 re-enters earth's atmosphere and plunges into the Indian Ocean at 10.21pm.
Monday *January 24*	First national water strike: 15,000 troops on standby!

Storms in the north

WATER STRIKE

Tuesday *January 25*	Shell fishing banned in the Wash by Boston council because of contaminated mussels.
Wednesday *January 26*	The Post Office issues new stamps: British River Fishes. A joint Anglo-American-Dutch infra-red space telescope is launched from Vandenburg Air Force base in California.

Red rain in the south of England

Thursday *January 27*	Princess Anne officially opens the new Save the Children Fund's Headquarters in Camberwell, London.

Friday *January 28*	Patrick Moore is named Pipeman of the Year and given a telescope-shaped pipe. Full Moon
Saturday *January 29*	The RSPB say that wild birds are so confused by the mild weather that some have started nesting!
Sunday *January 30*	Members of the English Civil War Society commemorate the execution of King Charles I (on January 30 1649) at the Banqueting Hall, Whitehall.
Monday *January 31*	The wearing of seat belts for drivers and front-seat passengers is compulsory from today.

The sunniest and mildest January in Aberdeen since records began

Happy Birthday Page!

850th anniversary of St Bartholomew's Fair in London
450th anniversary of Bristol Grammar School
100th anniversary of the Royal College of Music
100th anniversary of the parcel post
100th anniversary of the Boys' Brigade
75th anniversary of the Territorial Army
60th anniversary of BBC Children's Programmes
60th anniversary of the Flying Scotsman
50th anniversary of the British Film Institute
50th anniversary of King Kong
50th anniversary of the Royal Corgi
50th anniversary of London Transport
40th anniversary of the Royal Windsor Horse Show
25th anniversary of NASA
20th anniversary of Dr Who

DAILY GOSSIP 17p	HEDGEHOG ～ 20P	BLURB ～～～ 16p	THE DAILY FISH 18p
THE FREEDOM OF THE FALKLANDS FOR MRS THATCHER.	WATER STRIKE COMES TO BOIL!	IT'S PT FOR COMMUTERS AT WATERLOO WITH BBC BREAKFAST TIME TV!	PHONEY FIREBALL LANDS IN READING

February

Tuesday *February 1*	First day of TV-AM. The east coast is on full flood alert and the Thames Barrier is raised at 10pm in its first flood emergency.
Wednesday *February 2*	Thieves escape with more than 50kg of black puddings from a factory in Sherwood, Notts. The Thames Barrier is lowered at 6am.
Thursday *February 3*	A stuffed polar bear, more than 2m tall, and weighing 136kg, is stolen from a night club in Manchester.
Friday *February 4*	Dinky Toys Golden Jubilee Exhibition opens at the London Toy and Model Museum in London.
Saturday *February 5*	Snow has been diverted from Moscow this winter by aircraft dropping dry ice into the clouds as they approach the city. This brings the snow down sooner!
Sunday *February 6*	Steve Douce, 19, from Caterham in Surrey, becomes the new British Cyclo-Cross champion in Birmingham.
Monday *February 7*	David Hempleman-Adams sets out on an expedition to reach the North Pole alone, on foot.
Tuesday *February 8*	The racehorse Shergar, who won both the Irish and Epsom Derbys in 1981, and is worth £10,000,000, is kidnapped from a stud farm in Co. Kildare.
Wednesday *February 9*	The first £1 coin, which was struck by the Prince of Wales last April, is sold in aid of charity in London. It fetches £2,200!
Thursday *February 10*	Richard Broadhead, the only British yachtsman still in the single-handed round-the-world race, answers a distress call from a French yacht in the south Atlantic.
Friday *February 11*	First day of the 87th Crufts Dog Show in London. About 4,500 Little Auks are counted today at Whitburn Observatory near South Shields, blown off course by the gales.
Saturday *February 12*	Daley Thompson, who holds the world decathlon record with 8,744 points, injures his back while competing in a pentathlon in Toronto, Canada.
Sunday *February 13*	Beginning of the Chinese Year of the Pig.  New Moon
Monday *February 14*	Valentine's Day. Opening of an exhibition celebrating 60 years of BBC Children's Programmes—featuring Bill and Ben the Flowerpot Men, Andy Pandy and Muffin the Mule.

February

The Roman month of purification. The name comes from the Latin 'februo' which means 'I purify by sacrifice'. It has also been known as 'sprout kale' and 'rain month'.

The Pocket Money Page

The Pocket Money Monitor, an annual survey carried out by Gallup for Wall's Ice Cream, shows that children between the ages of 5 and 16 have had a raise of 29% in their pocket money during the last year! Although it varies slightly, according to where you live, and whether you are a girl or a boy, the average weekly pocket money is £1.22.

Pocket Money Table

Year	Total	Boys	Girls	5–7 yrs	8–10 yrs	11–13 yrs	14–16 yrs
1980	99p	99p	99p	59p	66p	109p	151.5p
1981	113p	117p	109p	55p	87p	122p	177p
1982	94.5p	93p	95.5p	64p	74p	113.5p	128p
1983	122p	124p	115p	90p	103p	141p	178p

Crutts 1983

A Pembroke Welsh Corgi called Belroyd Love Bird wins the Pup of the Year title. Montracia Kaskarak Hitarie, the first Afghan Hound ever to win the title, becomes Supreme Champion.

The Chinese Year of the Pig
February 13, 1983 – February 1, 1984

Pigs are gallant, trustworthy, truthful and confident!
They are also good sports, and good at working and making money. Female Pigs make excellent mothers. Pigs go well with Cats but not Snakes or Goats!
Famous Pigs include King Henry VIII and Oliver Cromwell.

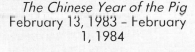

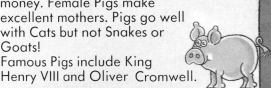

THE EAVESDROPPER 13p
SHERGAR HORSENAPPED!

LOUD HAILER 20p
LOST MEDIEVAL PALACE OF THE ARCH-BISHOPS OF CANTERBURY FOUND ON FRUIT FARM IN KENT

DAILY SCRIBBLE
FEBRUARY 9 – IT'S 'NO SMOKING' DAY

PEEP 16p
COSMOS 1441 GOES ROUND THE WORLD EVERY 97.5 MINUTES

Tuesday *February 15*	Pancake Day. The Kilauea volcano in Hawaii erupts again this week, with 6m lava fountains.
Wednesday *February 16*	Worst bush fires in Australian history last for 3 days. Russia launches Cosmos-1441, a satellite which will orbit earth every 97.5 minutes.
Thursday *February 17*	Interpol is called into the hunt for Shergar, the kidnapped race horse.
Friday *February 18*	Brian Baldry, the headmaster of Gazeley primary school, nr. Newmarket, Suffolk, wears sponsored shorts this week to raise money for the P.T.A.
Saturday *February 19*	Robert Calvert sets a new British altitude record, flying his microlight aircraft to 5867m in Lancashire.
Sunday *February 20*	A baby tarsier called E.T. is born at Stockholm Zoo, weighing 22.7gm and measuring 5cm.
Monday *February 21*	New food labelling regulations mean that a flounder may no longer be called a fluke, and rock salmon becomes rockfish or catfish!
Tuesday *February 22*	Thirty-day national water strike is called off. Lightning causes 80 new bush fires in Victoria, Australia.
Wednesday *February 23*	Gales in the North Sea wash thousands of sea birds ashore from the north of Scotland to Kent.
Thursday *February 24*	Happy 60th Birthday to the *Flying Scotsman*, which makes a celebration trip from the Steam Train Museum, Carnforth Steamtown, to Leeds.
Friday *February 25*	Fire destroys Birmingham's best-known landmark—the bull above the Bull Ring Shopping centre.
Saturday *February 26*	The Prince of Wales falls off his horse while hunting in Gloucestershire and gets 2 lovely black eyes.
Sunday *February 27*	International Magicians' Convention at Blackpool.
Monday *February 28*	Castle Rising in Norfolk is closed for a week so that the Mole Catcher can deal with a plague of moles.

Sharp night frosts

Full Moon

U.K. Fact File 1983

Total area of the United Kingdom — 244,099.7 sq. km

Capital City — London (157,9.9 sq.km: population 6,696,000)

Population of UK — 55,776,000

Females 28,701,000 Males 27,064.000

Members of Parliament 650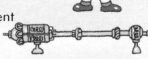

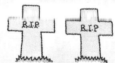 Births — 721,500

Marriages 389,300  Deaths 659,100

Most popular girls' name* — ELIZABETH | JAMES — Most popular boys' name*

Cub Scouts 295,000 Brownies 411,000  Scouts 229,000 Girl Guides 325,000

Licensed vehicles 20,216,000  Driving tests 1,892,300 (51.3% failed) Head of State Queen Elizabeth II

Prime Minister Margaret Hilda Thatcher

POEMS Poet Laureate Sir John Betjeman

Beautiful Britain Year

Astronomer Royal Prof. Francis Graham Smith

Boys' Brigade Year

International Giant Panda Year

UN's World Communications Year

GLC's Peace Year

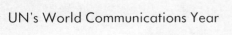

*according to *The Times* Newspaper's correspondence page

March

Tuesday *March 1*	St David's Day. A tornado and a mild earthquake in Los Angeles force the Queen to cancel her ride through the Santa Ynez mountains with President and Mrs Reagan.
Wednesday *March 2*	Lancelot, a Bewick Swan, leaves the Wildfowl Trust at Slimbridge, in Gloucestershire, after his 20th winter there. Cosmos-1443, an unmanned Soviet spacecraft, is launched.
Thursday *March 3*	Hergé (real name Georges Remi), the creator of *Tintin*, dies in Brussels, aged 75.
Friday *March 4*	David Hempleman-Adams, due to start his trek from Ward Hunt Island in Canada to the North Pole, is delayed by frozen batteries.
Saturday *March 5*	The Labour Party, led by Bob Hawke, wins the Australian general election.
Sunday *March 6*	The *Flying Scotsman*, making the most of its diamond jubilee, takes a trip from Peterborough to York.
Monday *March 7*	The Red Arrows aerobatics team says good-bye after 18 years to Cirencester, in Gloucestershire, with a farewell flypast. They are moving to Lincolnshire.
Tuesday *March 8*	The Ideal Home Exhibition opens in London with a special 12m-high replica of the Montgolfier brothers hot-air balloon, that made its first successful flight 200 years ago. A £1,000 note, issued in 1935, is sold for £6,800 at Christie's in London.
Wednesday *March 9*	*Bheema*, a baby rhino, is born at Whipsnade Park. David Hempleman-Adams starts his walk to the North Pole: the temperature is –30°C.
Thursday *March 10*	Soviet Cosmos-1443 launched 8 days ago, docks with orbiting space station Salyut-7.
Friday *March 11*	The Queen and the Duke of Edinburgh arrive back after their tour of the west coast of America and Canada.
Saturday *March 12*	Jayne Torvill and Christopher Dean achieve the first ever score of 9 maximum sixes in the history of figure skating and win their third successive World Ice Dance title in Helsinki.
Sunday *March 13*	Mothering Sunday. Eight postmen deliver flowers and chocolates in West Norfolk, the first Sunday special delivery since 1922.
Monday *March 14*	New Moon Commonwealth Day. Tadworth Court Hospital, the Surrey branch of the Great Ormond Street Hospital, is saved from closure.

March

Named after the Roman god Mars. It has also been known as 'rough-month', 'lengthening-month', 'boisterous-month' and 'windy-month'.

News Bubble!
First-ever crossing of the Mediterranean in a hot-air balloon! It took 21 hrs to fly from Ales in S. France to Rharsa in Tunisia 1198.7 kms.

Take Note!
£1,000 notes were first made in 1725 and were issued every few years for two centuries. They went out of use very gradually as cheque books became more common.

Bheema is the first Indian Rhino to be born at Whipsnade Park for more than 20 years. He weighs over 50kg.

Danger! Monster Repairs!

The dinosaurs in Crystal Palace Park in south London are being restored. They were built more than 130 years ago for Sir Joseph Paxton's Exhibition Centre.

March 9: The Post Office issues four new stamps to celebrate Commonwealth Day.

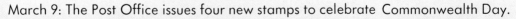

15½P COMMONWEALTH DAY 14 MARCH 1983

19½P COMMONWEALTH DAY 14 MARCH 1983

26P COMMONWEALTH DAY 14 MARCH 1983

29P COMMONWEALTH DAY 14 MARCH 1983

Tuesday *March 15*	Budget Day. Child benefit goes up by 11% in November, from £5.85 to £6.50.
Wednesday *March 16*	David Hempleman-Adams is airlifted back to base camp after covering only 16kms of his journey to the North Pole. His tent was torn, his sleeping bag was drenched and the temperature is –45°C!
Thursday *March 17*	St Patrick's Day. Volunteers rescue frogs and spawn from marshes which are going to be filled in and redeveloped at Bracknell, Berks.
Friday *March 18*	Prince William of Wales (9 months) leaves for a 6-week tour of Australia and New Zealand. With him go his parents, two nannies, his own policeman, teddy and cuddly toys.
Saturday *March 19*	David Livingstone, the Scottish missionary and traveller, was born on this day in 1813.
Sunday *March 20*	Wayne Dickinson breaks the record for the smallest boat to cross the Atlantic when his yacht *God's Tear* (2.7m) lands in Ireland. David Hempleman-Adams sets off to walk to the North Pole again!
Monday *March 21*	The Prince and Princess of Wales broadcast to the world's largest classroom in the outback of Australia—the Alice Springs School of the Air!
Tuesday *March 22*	Severe drought in Ethiopia: 2,000,000 people need emergency aid.
Wednesday *March 23*	The new £5,250,000 Henry Cole Wing is opened at the Victoria and Albert Museum in London: one of its galleries has solar-controlled blinds.
Thursday *March 24*	In Rome the Pantheon, temple to all the gods, is closed after a chunk of plaster falls from the ceiling.
Friday *March 25*	Nicola Cording (10) performs police duty in Downing Street—thanks to BBC's 'Jim'll Fix It'. Eighteen Indian cobras hatch at London Zoo.
Saturday *March 26*	Liverpool becomes the first football club to win the League/Milk Cup 3 times running when they beat Manchester United at Wembley.
Sunday *March 27*	Summer Time begins at 1am GMT. Watch out for Giant Hogweed, which grows up to 4m high with leaves more than 1m wide, on river banks and road and railway embankments!

Monday *March 28*	U.S. rescue satellite, Sarsat, is launched to locate ships and aircraft in distress. A new crater opens on Mount Etna, in Sicily, and lava pours down the eastern side. Full Moon
Tuesday *March 29*	An RAF Vulcan bomber flies low over Manchester to mark the opening of the new £2,000,000 Air and Space Museum.
Wednesday *March 30*	The count-down begins for the launch of the new space shuttle Challenger for take-off next Monday from Cape Canaveral. Four cheetah cubs, (Zero, Zake, Zena and Zara) are born at Whipsnade Park.
Thursday *March 31*	Maundy Service at Exeter Cathedral: the Queen distributes specially-minted money to 57 women and 57 men. The numbers match her age—she will be 57 on April 21.

Top Ten Names 1983*

1) Elizabeth (1)
2) Louise (2)
3) Jane (3)
4) Mary (4)
5) Charlotte (8)
6) Victoria (7)
7) Sarah (6)
8) Alice (9)
9) Katherine (5)
10) Alexandra (10)
     Emily (12)

1) James (1)
2) William (3)
3) Edward (2)
4) Alexander (4)
5) Thomas (5)
6) Charles (7)
7) John (6)
8) David (9)
9) Richard (10)
10) Robert (8)

The figures in brackets show the position in 1982.

*according to *The Times* newspaper's correspondence page.

DAILY OWL 18p

LETTER BOMB IS SENT TO 10 DOWNING STREET

THE NOSEY PARKER

21p

GIANT PANDAS MATE AT WASHINGTON ZOO

SCOOP 20p

'THE SNOWMAN' AND 'BOOK-TOWER' WIN BRITISH ACADEMY AWARDS

DAILY TRUMPET 16p

HERGÉ, THE CREATOR OF TINTIN, DIES AT 75

April

Friday *April 1*	April Fools' Day and Good Friday. British Marbles Championships start at Tinsley Green, West Sussex.
Saturday *April 2*	Oxford wins its eighth successive University Boat Race by 4½ lengths in 19 mins 0.07 secs.
Sunday *April 3*	Easter Sunday. Easter Egg Hunt at Leeds Castle in Kent: 5,000 chocolate eggs are hidden in the undergrowth!
Monday *April 4*	Bank Holiday. Beginning of Scout Job Week. America's second space shuttle, Challenger, is launched from Cape Canaveral in Florida, carrying 4 astronauts on a 5-day mission.
Tuesday *April 5*	First class letters go up from 15½ pence to 16 pence. Second class stay at 12½ pence.
Wednesday *April 6*	A 25.6m gorilla balloon is inflated on top of the Empire State Building in New York to celebrate the 50th anniversary of the film *King Kong*.
Thursday *April 7*	Two of the shuttle astronauts take the first American spacewalk for 9 years. They spend nearly 4 hours outside Challenger.
Friday *April 8*	Richard and Adrian Crane, who left Darjeeling on March 18 to run 4,000km along the Himalayas, set off on the second leg of their journey from Katmandu, after a 2-day rest.
Saturday *April 9*	Corbière wins the Grand National at Aintree to become the first horse trained by a woman (Jenny Pitman) to win the race.
Sunday *April 10*	A Force 8 gale and high tide flood Chesil Beach at Portland, Dorset.
Monday *April 11*	Police seal off the Embankment in London after dredging up a World War II German bomb from the river Thames near Waterloo Bridge.
Tuesday *April 12*	The film *E.T.*, which has broken all box office records, wins 4 Oscars.
Wednesday *April 13*	Rare Animal VC, awarded to a pigeon called Mercury during World War II, is sold at Christie's in London. New Moon
Thursday *April 14*	The first cordless telephone is launched.

The opening month – from the Latin 'aperire' which means to open. Also known as the time of budding.

Mercury's Medal

The Animal VC is properly known as the Dickin Medal, named after Maria Dickin, who founded the PDSA (People's Dispensary for Sick Animals). Only 53 of these very special medals were ever awarded, between 1942 and 1949, to 31 pigeons, 18 dogs, 3 horses and 1 cat. Mercury, who was 5 years old, received her award for 'the most outstanding single performance' of any one pigeon on special service section. She was one of 100 birds selected for a top-secret mission during the last war; they were all parachuted into enemy-occupied territory. Mercury flew back non-stop 770km over the North Sea, with a message from members of the Danish Resistance in July 1942. She was the only bird to return.

£1 coin: the vital statistics

Weight: 9.5 grams
Diameter: 22.5 mms
Edge thickness: 3.1 mms
Composition: 70% copper
                5.5% nickel
                24.5% zinc

Round the edge is a special Latin inscription which used to be written on golden guineas in the time of King Charles II.

Bones to Newmarket

Eclipse was one of the greatest race horses of all times. His skeleton used to live in the Natural History Museum in London but has been moved to Newmarket this month for the opening of the new National Horseracing Museum.

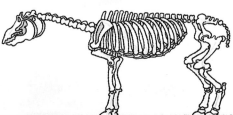

Friday *April 15*	David Hempleman-Adams abandons his attempt to walk to the North Pole, after being trapped in his tent 290km from the Pole for 4 days in ferocious blizzards.
Saturday *April 16*	The monster King Kong balloon on top of the Empire State Building in New York is under repair: it blew against the side and punctured itself.
Sunday *April 17*	The London Marathon is open to professionals for the first time. Michael Gratton (England) wins in 2hrs 9mins 43secs and Grete Waltz (Norway) equals the world's best time for women in 2hrs 25mins 29secs.
Monday *April 18*	The Princess of Wales rubs noses with Susan Piper — a traditional Maori form of welcome — in Auckland, New Zealand.

 12.8hrs of sunshine at Cape Wrath, Scotland

Tuesday *April 19*	A python, stolen from London Zoo, is found in a gentlemen's lavatory at Fenchurch Street Station.

Snow in Scotland and northern Ireland

Wednesday *April 20*	Three Soviet cosmonauts are launched in Soyuz T-8 to join the orbiting space station, Salyut-7.
Thursday *April 21*	The Queen's birthday. The new £1 coin goes into circulation.
Friday *April 22*	Three Soviet cosmonauts return safely to earth, having failed to dock with the orbiting space station, Salyut-7.
Saturday *April 23*	St George's Day. Shakespeare's birthday (1564) and the day he died (1616). Luxembourg wins the Eurovision Song Contest.
Sunday *April 24*	Chu-in, a 7-month-old panda, gets stuck up a tree at Madrid Zoo, and has to be rescued by keepers!
Monday *April 25*	The wettest April in central London since records began in 1940.

 Mild earthquake in southern Italy

Tuesday *April 26*	A one-man yellow submarine, built by Arthur Johnson of Grimsby, is sold for £1,400. It made a guest appearance at the premiere of the Beatles film *The Yellow Submarine*.

Wednesday *April 27*	A games mistress in Derby is struck by lightning while playing rounders and survives because she is wearing rubber-soled shoes. Full Moon
Thursday *April 28*	Jayne Torvill and Christopher Dean, the World Ice Dance champions, are made Honorary Freemen of the city of Nottingham.
Friday *April 29*	Thamesdown Borough Council in Swindon bans fox-hunting on its land.
Saturday *April 30*	The Queen opens the New National Horseracing Museum at Newmarket.

TOP TEN FILMS 1983
(according to *Screen International*)

1) E.T.
2) Return of the Jedi
3) Octopussy
4) Gandhi
5) Tootsie
6) Superman III
7) An Officer and a Gentleman
8) Staying Alive
9) Airplane II
10) The Meaning of Life

TOP TEN SPORTS 1983
(according to the Sports Council)

1) Walking
2) Outdoor swimming
3) Indoor swimming
4) Billiards
5) Snooker
6) Angling
7) Golf
8) Soccer
9) Lawn tennis
10) Table tennis

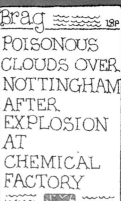

The Grapevine
THE FIRST HEARING DOG GOES TO WORK

17p

SQUIGGLE
20P

IT'S A STEAL! £7,000,000 ROBBERY IN LONDON

DAILY SNOOP
15p

SPIDERMAN, SUPERMAN AND 2 SKELETONS RUN IN LONDON MARATHON

Brag
18p

POISONOUS CLOUDS OVER NOTTINGHAM AFTER EXPLOSION AT CHEMICAL FACTORY

May

Sunday *May 1*	A Hudsonian Godwit, in full summer plumage, makes a rare visit from North America to the Blacktoft Sands nature reserve, nr. Goole, Humberside.
Monday *May 2*	Bank Holiday. Beautiful Britain Day—to launch Beautiful Britain Year! More than 3,000 runners take part in the Belfast marathon: Paul Craig (25) wins in record time of 2hrs 20mins 14secs.
Tuesday *May 3*	George Alcock (70) spots a new comet in the north-east sky from the landing of his home near Peterborough.
Wednesday *May 4*	The Queen opens the Wall Walk at the Tower of London.
Thursday *May 5*	An animal believed to be a puma is sighted at the RAF Halton housing estate at Wendover in Buckinghamshire. It leaves paw-prints 12.7cm in diameter.
Friday *May 6*	Today is National Stamp Day: the anniversary of the issue of the first postage stamp, the Penny Black, in 1840.
Saturday *May 7*	Mrs Linda Chalker, Transport Under-Secretary, passes her Advanced Motorists' driving test.
Sunday *May 8*	Christopher Hughes (34), a London Underground Train driver, becomes BBC's Mastermind of 1983.
Monday *May 9*	Mrs Thatcher announces that there will be a General Election on June 9.
Tuesday *May 10*	The 500-year-old Major Oak, where Robin Hood hid in Sherwood Forest, is budding—only 9 months after it was badly damaged by fire.
Wednesday *May 11*	Schoolgirl, Gabrielle Malloy (16), is the youngest-ever winner of the Super Brain of Britain competition in Birmingham. Alcock's Comet (see May 3) comes to within 4,600,000kms of earth—closer than any other comet since 1770.
Thursday *May 12*	A 190kg lioness escapes from a circus in Didcot, Oxfordshire, but is quickly recaptured. New Moon
Friday *May 13*	There are more kangaroos than people in Australia—about 19,000,000, compared with 15,000,000 people!
Saturday *May 14*	Cowpat-hurling contest near Leatherhead in Surrey, organised by Surrey Young Farmers.

May

Takes its name from Maia, the goddess of growth and increase, or from 'maiores', the Latin word for elders, who were honoured this month. The Anglo-Saxons called it 'thrimilce' because cows could be milked three times a day now. An Old Dutch name was 'bloumaand' which means blossoming month.

Comet-Spotter-In-Chief

George Alcock has spotted four comets since 1959. They have all been named after him! In 1979 he was awarded the MBE for services to astronomy.

Help!

Britain's smallest nature reserve near Cheltenham in Gloucestershire is in danger from a road and housing development. Also threatened is one of the country's rarest plants which grows nowhere else—the RANUNCULUS OPHIOGLOSSIFOLIUS—known as the Badgeworth buttercup or adder's tongue spearwort!

Mount Etna

Lava has been flowing down Mount Etna in Sicily for weeks. It is the highest and most active volcano in Europe—with more than 135 recorded eruptions! There were 16 during the 18th century and 19 during the 19th. More recently, there was a series of violent eruptions in 1950 and 1951—believed to be the strongest for 200 years.

Sabi's Birthday Cake
(The Original and Genuine Recipe from Howlett's Zoo)

6.3 kg currants
2.2 kg apricots
2.2 kg prunes
5.4 kg bananas

Sunday *May 15*	The Wheelchair Ten Tors Expedition on Dartmoor—156 children take part. The routes vary in length between 9.6km and 24.1km.
Monday *May 16*	The first wheel clamps appear in central London. A brown Mercedes in Sloane Street is the first victim at 11.58am. It costs £19.50 on top of the parking penalty to get a car released.
Tuesday *May 17*	The post of Lord Mayor is abolished by Liverpool Council.
Wednesday *May 18*	Pope John Paul II was born in 1920. London has its 32nd consecutive day of rain.
Thursday *May 19*	The southbound carriageway of the M3 at Basingstoke in Hampshire is blocked by apples, when a lorry sheds its load.
Friday *May 20*	The American space shuttle, Enterprise, on its way to the Paris Air Show and on the back of a Boeing 747, calls in at RAF Fairford, Gloucestershire, to refuel.
Saturday *May 21*	102nd FA Cup Final at Wembley: Manchester United and Brighton draw 2–2 after extra time.
Sunday *May 22*	Whit Sunday. The 12-day bicycle Milk Race starts at Bournemouth.
Monday *May 23*	The batteries on Viking 1, the spacecraft which landed on Mars in 1976, and were only guaranteed for 90 days, finally run out.
Tuesday *May 24*	A tiny Oxo van made in 1924 fetches £500 at Sotheby's in London—a record price for a Dinky toy!
Wednesday *May 25*	Three new stamps are issued by the Post Office to celebrate engineering achievements. Happy first birthday to Sabi, the African elephant at Howlett's Zoo near Canterbury in Kent!
Thursday *May 26*	Manchester United beats Brighton 4–0 in the FA Cup Final replay. Full Moon Earthquake (7.7 on the Richter Scale) and tidal wave in Japan
Friday *May 27*	The Prince and Princess of Wales visit the Duchy of Cornwall. Amelia Bloomer, famous campaigner for women's rights and designer of the bloomer, was born in New York, 1818.

Saturday *May 28*	Thieves break into Dulwich College Art Gallery in London and again steal a Rembrandt painting which has been stolen 3 times in the past 15 years. Five Snowy Owls (4 females and 1 male) hatch at London Zoo.
Sunday *May 29*	British Human Catapault Championships at Ratcliff-on-Soar, near Nottingham. A volcano erupts under Europe's largest glacier, the Vatnajökull, in south-east Iceland.
Monday *May 30*	Bank Holiday. Blue Peter's 7-year-old tabby cat, Jill, who appeared in 587 programmes, dies.
Tuesday *May 31*	Four hundred canoeists (aged 12–19), who set off from Shrewsbury on Saturday on a 160km journey down the river Severn, arrive at Wainloads Hill, near Gloucester.

TOP TEN SINGLES 1983
(according to the *New Musical Express*)

1) Blue Monday (New Order)
2) Karma Chameleon (Culture Club)
3) I.O.U. (Freeze)
3) Red Red Wine (UB40)
5) Billi Jean (Michael Jackson)
6) Wherever I Lay My Hat (Paul Young)
7) Let's Dance (David Bowie)
8) Uptown Girl (Billy Joel)
9) Every Breath You Take (Police)
   Flashdance . . . What a Feeling (Irene Cara)

TOP TEN SINGLES ARTISTES 1983
(according to the *New Musical Express*)

1) Culture Club
2) Wham!
3) Michael Jackson
4) Eurythmics
5) David Bowie
6) Paul Young
7) Style Council
8) Spandau Ballet
9) Madness
10) New Order

May 25: The Post Office issues 3 new stamps celebrating engineering achievements.

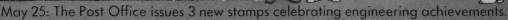

THE BELLOWS 18p
500 DIE AS NILE STEAMER SINKS IN CROCODILE — INFESTED WATERS

DAILY HOOT 20p
SPECIAL SPAGHETTI WHEAT TO BE SOWN IN THE MIDLANDS AND THE SOUTH

BUGLER 16p
BLOOD SAMPLE CARRIER PIGEONS AXED AS HOSPITAL CLOSES IN DEVONPORT

HONK 19p
PRISONERS TAKE OVER TWO WINGS OF ALBANY PRISON ON ISLE OF — WIGHT

June

Wednesday *June 1*	International Children's Day. Lester Piggot wins his ninth Derby at Epsom in 2min 49.07secs.
Thursday *June 2*	A 62-gun salute from the Tower of London marks the 30th anniversary of the Queen's Coronation. An unmanned Soviet spacecraft, Venera 15, is launched: it should go into orbit around Venus in October. *Return of the Jedi* opens in London.
Friday *June 3*	A slug-guard is mounted in Oxfordshire on the only known military orchid growing wild in Britain!
Saturday *June 4*	Daley Thompson loses his world decathlon record to Jurgen Hinsen of West Germany by 34 points.
Sunday *June 5*	The American space shuttle, Enterprise, goes on show at Stansted Airport in Essex.
Monday *June 6*	About 1000 cars have been clamped in central London since the scheme started on May 16. Diplomats at the French Embassy in Knightsbridge are top of the league with 11 clampings!
Tuesday *June 7*	A young porpoise is rescued in the river Don at Doncaster after swimming 128km inland from the sea. It is released into the sea at Bridlington. Another unmanned Soviet spacecraft, Venera 16, starts its journey to Venus.
Wednesday *June 8*	An escaped llama causes chaos on a main road near Bath!
Thursday *June 9*	General Election. Tom McLean sails from St Johns, Newfoundland in *Giltspur* (2.3m), in an attempt to win back the record for sailing across the Atlantic in the smallest craft.
Friday *June 10*	The General Election results in a landslide victory: Conservatives 397 seats; Labour 209; Liberals 17; Social Democrats 6; Plaid Cymru 2; Scottish Nationalists 2; others 17.
Saturday *June 11*	The Queen's official birthday is marked by Trooping the Colour on Horseguards' Parade. New Moon
Sunday *June 12*	Twelfth International Birdman Rally at Bognor Regis in Sussex. Competitors try to fly 50 metres off the end of the pier to win £3,000, but no one manages it.
Monday *June 13*	Pioneer 10, a 1/4-tonne spacecraft which was launched in 1972, leaves the solar system and speeds on to interstellar space.

June

Takes its name from the great goddess Juno, or from *juniores*, the Latin word for young people, who were honoured this month. 'Zomer-maand' in Old Dutch (summer month) and 'Seremonath' in Old Saxon (dry month).

Star Films

The third 'Star Wars' film *Return of the Jedi* took £1,786,977 in the first fortnight! The first in the series, *Star Wars*, made in 1977, took £349,000,000 altogether, and *The Empire Strikes Back*, made in 1980, took £243,000,000!

STAR TRAVELLER

Pioneer 10 carries a message from mankind on board as it speeds into deepest space—just in case it encounters any extra-terrestrial life who want to know where it came from! A series of scientific symbols, a map of the nine planets and a picture of a naked couple are engraved on a special plaque. The spacecraft was launched 12 years ago and is still transmitting messages back to earth, although it is so far away that they take $4\frac{1}{2}$ hours to get here!

STAR RUNNERS

Richard and Adrian Crane from Keswick in Cumbria cross 64 passes in their run along the Himalayas. Altogether, they climb about 91,440m—more than 10 times the height of Mount Everest—over some of the roughest terrain in the world! They each lose over 6kg on the 3,265km run.

DAILY WHOOP 21p

HUGE HAILSTONES DAMAGE CROPS—8000 PANES OF GLASS BROKEN AT ONE NURSERY NEAR BOGNOR, SUSSEX

THE WORLD 18p

300 YEAR OLD NAVAL DOCKYARD TO CLOSE IN CHATHAM

CLANGERS 19p
'O LEVELS AND 'CSE' TO MAKE WAY FOR 'GCSE'

SENSATION 15p
PEOPLES MARCH FOR JOBS REACHES LONDON — UNEMPLOYED NOW OVER 3,000,000

Tuesday *June 14*	The Prince and Princess of Wales leave Heathrow for a tour of Canada. Buzby, the British Telecom bird, retires after 8 years.
Wednesday *June 15*	Peter Bird, who rowed across the Pacific in 10 months, arrives at a naval base in North Queensland, Australia, having been rescued from the Great Barrier Reef.
Thursday *June 16*	Ten young sea eagles arrive in Scotland from Norway on board an RAF Nimrod aircraft. They are *en route* for a nature reserve on the Island of Rhum.
Friday *June 17*	Penelop Wyman (10), who saved her pocket money and sent chocolate bars to everyone on board *HMS Penelope* in the Falklands, visits the ship in Devonport today.
Saturday *June 18*	Dr Sally Ride, the first American woman in space, blasts off in the shuttle, Challenger, with 4 other astronauts. Also on board – 151 carpenter ants, including their Queen, Norma.
Sunday *June 19*	Colin Gumbrell (21) from Horsham, Sussex, scores 1612 points in 3 games and wins the National Scrabble Championship in London.
Monday *June 20*	Dial 0101-307-410-6272 to hear the shuttle astronauts talking to Mission Control! Two jaguar cubs, Domino and Dice, are born at Whipsnade Park.
Tuesday *June 21*	Longest day of the year. Happy first birthday to Prince William of Wales!
Wednesday *June 22*	State Opening of Parliament. The Queen takes 9mins to deliver her speech.
Thursday *June 23*	Lynn Dickens floats across Llangorse Lake, near Brecon in Powys, in a giant polythene bubble as high as a 5-storey office block!
Friday *June 24*	Midsummer's Day. The space shuttle Challenger lands perfectly at Edwards Air Force Base in California, after 6 days and 98 orbits of the earth.
Saturday *June 25*	Joss Naylor, the 'flying shepherd', sets out to run past every mere, water and lake in the Lake District to break the record of 25½ hours set last year. Full Moon
Sunday *June 26*	The eighth London to Brighton Bike Ride. 12,000 cyclists take part in aid of the British Heart Foundation.

Monday *June 27*	Two British brothers, Richard and Adrian Crane, complete a record 101-day run along the Himalayas from Darjeeling to Rawalpindi.
Tuesday *June 28*	Two Soviet cosmonauts, launched yesterday aboard a Soyuz T-9 spacecraft, dock with the orbiting space station, Salyut-7.
Wednesday *June 29*	Shigechiyo Izumi, who is listed as the oldest person in the world by the *Guinness Book of Records*, celebrates his 118th birthday in Japan.
Thursday *June 30*	An extra 'leap' second is added to the last minute of today to make up for the slight irregularity of the earth's rotation.

The Changing Face of 1983

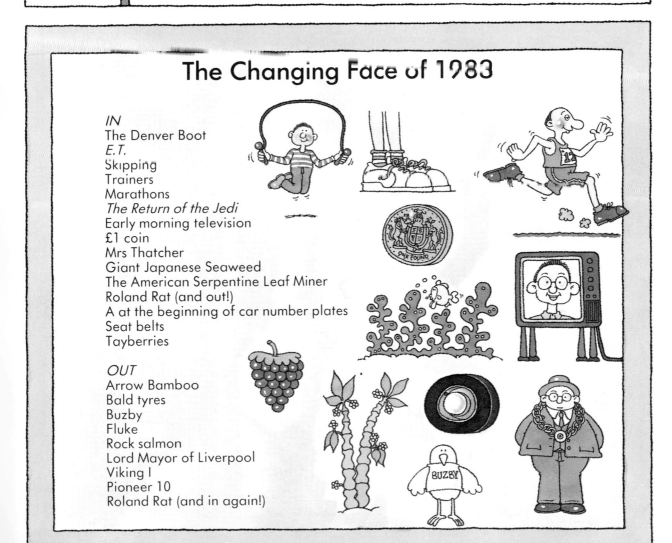

IN
The Denver Boot
E.T.
Skipping
Trainers
Marathons
The Return of the Jedi
Early morning television
£1 coin
Mrs Thatcher
Giant Japanese Seaweed
The American Serpentine Leaf Miner
Roland Rat (and out!)
A at the beginning of car number plates
Seat belts
Tayberries

OUT
Arrow Bamboo
Bald tyres
Buzby
Fluke
Rock salmon
Lord Mayor of Liverpool
Viking I
Pioneer 10
Roland Rat (and in again!)

July

Friday *July 1*	Sixty-five thousand people sing Happy Birthday to the Princess of Wales (22 today) at the opening of the World University Games in Edmonton, Canada.
Saturday *July 2*	Martina Navratilova wins the ladies' singles and the ladies' doubles titles at the Wimbledon Lawn Tennis Championships.
Sunday *July 3*	John McEnroe wins the men's singles title at Wimbledon. Yachtsman Mike Spring, paralysed from the waist down, completes a solo voyage to the Azores in 16 days.
Monday *July 4*	The House of Lords discuss a report about children and television: on average, children aged 5–14 watch TV for 23 hours a week!
Tuesday *July 5*	Three young otters, bred at the Otter Trust in Suffolk, are released into the wild in an attempt to rebuild the otter population on the Norfolk and Suffolk Broads.
Wednesday *July 6*	The Post Office issues new stamps showing British Army uniforms. The largest strawberry recorded in the UK has been grown by George Andersen in his allotment at Folkestone, Kent. It weighs over 227gm (8.17oz)!
Thursday *July 7*	The Queen Mother visits the United Biscuits factory in Harlesden, North London.
Friday *July 8*	Heatwave! 28°C at Liphook in Hampshire and Cardiff. Twenty elephants have to be rescued from a flooded circus in West Germany after violent thunderstorms.
Saturday *July 9*	A new lifeboat goes on station at Whitstable in Kent. It is called the *British Diver* after members of the British Sub-Aqua Club, who raised £23,000 to buy it.
Sunday *July 10*	Eight pythons, 2 boa constrictors and 4 large lizards escape from a pet shop in Peckham, London. Jellyfish up to 30cm in diameter invade Lincolnshire beaches. New Moon
Monday *July 11*	Two policemen from Cambridge parascend under 10 Thames bridges, from Lambeth to Tower Bridge, to raise money for the Hospital for Sick Children, Great Ormond Street.
Tuesday *July 12*	Tom McLean, who left Newfoundland 33 days ago to cross the Atlantic in *Giltspur* (2.3m), is about 965km from Falmouth, Cornwall, now.

Wednesday *July 13*	The heatwave continues: twelve people collapse at a garden party at Buckingham Palace. It's the hottest day in London since 1976 with temperatures of 31°C. Gemma Plant (3) from Leek, Staffordshire, wins the Miss Pears contest.
Thursday *July 14*	It is so hot that judges are allowed to remove their wigs in the High Courts!
Friday *July 15*	St Swithin's Day. The Festival Pier, outside the Festival Hall in London, is officially opened.
Saturday *July 16*	The Tayberry is launched. A cross between a blackberry, a raspberry and a loganberry, it was developed at the British Research Institute on Tayside — which explains its name!
Sunday *July 17*	The annual London-Calais-London Powerboat Race sets off from *HMS Belfast* near Tower Bridge.
Monday *July 18*	The new Penlee lifeboat in Cornwall is named *Mabel Alice*. A herd of seals is stranded in the river Welland at Spalding in Lincolnshire. Michael Read (42), from Suffolk, swims the Channel for the 27th time – in 18hrs 13mins!

July

 Named in honour of Julius Caesar. The Old Dutch name was 'Hooy-maand' (hay month) and the Old Saxon name was 'Maedd-monath' because the cattle were turned into the meadow to feed.

Claws!

'The most important find this century!'

Baryonyx walkeri, a new 124,000,000-year-old flesh-eating dinosaur was found in a claypit in Surrey, near Gatwick airport, on Friday, January 7. It took 8 people 3 weeks to excavate the skeleton after William Walker found the first enormous clawbone. The Natural History Museum in London have called it the most important and exciting discovery this century! Baryonyx is from the Greek meaning 'heavy claw' and walkeri is in honour of William Walker.

Tuesday *July 19*	The Natural History Museum announces the discovery of a huge clawbone from a 124-million-year-old dinosaur in a claypit near Gatwick airport in Surrey.
Wednesday *July 20*	Salvation Army Commissioner Catherine Bramwell Booth celebrates her 100th birthday. A black face appears for the first time on a South African stamp.
Thursday *July 21*	First men landed on the moon in 1969. An earthquake close to the Mt Etna volcano shakes Sicily. Earth tremors in north-east Italy as well.
Friday *July 22*	Giant Japanese seaweed, known as *Sargassum Muticum*, has rounded Land's End from the English Channel.
Saturday *July 23*	Hailstones the size of marbles break car windscreens at Okehampton, Devon.
Sunday *July 24*	A two-toed sloth is born at Bristol Zoo. Fifty competitors take part in the Round London Air Race. Full Moon
Monday *July 25*	Matthew Webb drowned trying to swim across Niagara Falls, 100 yrs ago today.
Tuesday *July 26*	A 2-year-old racing pigeon, which flew off course to Canada when it should have been flying from Penzance to Manchester, returns to Heathrow by plane. An 800-tonne Spanish cargo ship collides with the new Thames Barrier.
Wednesday *July 27*	Tina, a 2-tonne circus elephant, takes her morning walk along the beach at Bournemouth. A tiny meteorite has chipped a window of the orbiting Soviet space station, Salyut-7.
Thursday *July 28*	The heatwave in Europe continues: forest fires in Italy, car washing banned in Germany!
Friday *July 29*	Hottest month for more than 100 years in London, Plymouth and Durham.
Saturday *July 30*	Happy Birthday, Daley Thompson! 25 today! A crocodile (1.8m) leaps into a fishing boat near Darwin in North Australia, bites a man's shoulder and jumps back into the water.
Sunday *July 31*	The first Inventors' Day at Longleat House in Wiltshire: more than 120 inventions are on display, including a walking device for goldfish, an electronic mousetrap, a welly wiper and an electric garden spade.

August

Monday *August 1*	A at the beginning of car number plates from today – instead of Y at the end! Parcel post came into operation 100 years ago today.
Tuesday *August 2*	The outline of the Cerne Giant, the huge figure cut into the chalk hill above Cerne Abbas in Dorset, is sharpened up by the British Trust for Conservation.
Wednesday *August 3*	Mrs Thatcher has an emergency operation on her right eye.
Thursday *August 4*	Happy 83rd Birthday to Queen Elizabeth the Queen Mother! Alison Streeter becomes the first woman to swim the Channel both ways non-stop. It takes her 21hrs 16mins.
Friday *August 5*	Moby Dick, a white whale, finds his way out of shallow waters in the Lim Fjord in Denmark, having been trapped for 3 months. Then he gets trapped in a salmon net.
Saturday *August 6*	First Athletics World Championships opens in Helsinki 159 nations take part. Bill Neal, from Salcombe in Devon, enters the Danish National Bathtub Race in Copenhagen.
Sunday *August 7*	Jaws! A great white shark, measuring 5m and weighing over 1000kg, is caught in Long Island Sound, USA.
Monday *August 8*	Carl Lewis (USA) wins the 100m title at Helsinki. New Moon
Tuesday *August 9*	There has been no rain on Lundy in the Bristol Channel for over 2 months: the 18 people who live there are asked to wash in the sea.
Wednesday *August 10*	Tom McLean lands at Oporto in Portugal, having crossed the Atlantic in a record 62 days in his yacht *Giltspur* (2.3m). Carl Lewis (USA) wins the long jump, and helps to set a world record in the 4 × 100m relay in Helsinki.
Thursday *August 11*	80,000 homes and offices in Southampton are without electricity after a doves' nest causes an explosion at a sub-station.
Friday *August 12*	The Perseid meteor shower is at its best tonight! Oriental Small-clawed Otter born at London Zoo.
Saturday *August 13*	Twenty-three Red Kites, one of Britain's rarest birds, have been successfully reared this season in Wales. Daley Thompson (GB) wins the decathlon with 8666 points in Helsinki.

Sunday *August 14*	Special US space stamps ($9.35) are issued for letters which will orbit earth on board the next space shuttle flight. Steve Cram wins the 1500m in Helsinki.
Monday *August 15*	Restoration work begins on the steeple of St Mary-le-Strand in London, and on Shrewsbury Station in Shropshire.
Tuesday *August 16*	The average Briton drinks 1650 cups of tea every year, or just under 4½ cups a day.
Wednesday *August 17*	More than 5000 chickens are shed onto the Tyne Bridge in Newcastle by a lorry.
Thursday *August 18*	Samantha Druce (12), from Dorset, becomes the youngest girl to swim the Channel.
Friday *August 19*	Ruth Lawrence (12), who is going to Oxford University in October, passes Physics 'A' Level with grade A.
Saturday *August 20*	Announcing the new Dr Who: Colin Baker! The American Everest Expedition pitch base camp at 5475m on their way up to the West Ridge.
Sunday *August 21*	Richard Crane (29), who finished running along the Himalayas on June 27, wins the first Quadrathon in 16hrs 26mins 49secs.
Monday *August 22*	The Great Clock of Westminster (Big Ben) is hidden by scaffolding and plastic sheeting—part of a 6-year renovation of the Palace of Westminster.
Tuesday *August 23*	Haringey Council get planning permission to rebuild Alexandra Palace, which burned down in 1980. New Moon
Wednesday *August 24*	The Post Office issue 4 new stamps to celebrate British Gardens. Sarah-Jane Hutt, from Poole in Dorset, is crowned Miss UK Vesuvius erupted in AD 79. Earthquake in north-west California
Thursday *August 25*	New British free-fall parachute record of 8321m is set at Sibson, near Peterborough. Kalli, a mongrel dog, is fostering two 5-week-old puma cubs at Guilsborough Wildlife Park, near Northampton.
Friday *August 26*	Happy 24th Birthday to the Mini, which is still being produced at more than 1000 a week at Longbridge. Cutty Sark Tall Ships Race from Weymouth to St Malo.

August

Named in honour of the Roman Emperor Augustus, whose lucky month it was. The Old Dutch name was 'Oost-maand' – harvest month. The Old Saxon name was 'Weod-monath' – weed month.

Pandas

1. About 100 Giant Pandas live in the Wolong Reserve in Sichuan.

2. It is the largest and most important Panda Reserve in China.

3. Pandas' favourite food is Arrow Bamboo. An adult can eat nearly 15kg a day!

4. But the Arrow Bamboo is flowering now, which only happens once every 50 or 60 years.

5. This means that it is inedible for the Pandas. After flowering, the bamboo withers and dies.

6. This means that the Pandas face starvation.

7. The Chinese Government has launched a special programme to save the Pandas. And given £100,000 to help feed them.

The Quadrathon

3.2 km swim
51.5 km walk

160.9 km cycle ride
41.8 km marathon

BLAH 18p

THE QUEEN MUM IS 83

CHIT-CHAT 20p

BLIND MAN SAILS ACROSS THE PACIFIC SINGLE-HANDED

FREDS NEWS 16p

RADIO CAROLINE RETURNS TO THE AIRWAVES. THE PREVIOUS SHIP SANK 3 YEARS AGO

DAILY COMET 17p

JAWS IS CAUGHT IN LONG ISLAND SOUND

Saturday *August 27*	A new exhibition to mark the centenary of the eruption of the volcano at Krakatoa opens at the Natural History Museum in London.
Sunday *August 28*	For Sale: bricks from the Cavern Club in Liverpool – made famous by the Beatles. Price: £5 each.
Monday *August 29*	Bank Holiday. Mike Spring, who is paralysed in both legs, arrives in Penzance, after a 4000km journey to the Azores and back in his yacht *3M Mariner*.
Tuesday *August 30*	US space shuttle, Challenger, is launched from Cape Canaveral in Florida, with a 4-man crew, including America's first black astronaut. Also on board are 260,000 stamped envelopes—the first space letters!
Wednesday *August 31*	Russell Doig, of Stanwell, Middlesex, receives a trophy for hooking the first salmon in the river Thames for 150 years.

August 24: The Post Office issues four new stamps to celebrate British Gardens.

20TH CENTURY GARDEN
SISSINGHURST

19TH CENTURY GARDEN
BIDDULPH GRANGE

18TH CENTURY GARDEN
BLENHEIM

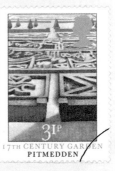
17TH CENTURY GARDEN
PITMEDDEN

Krakatoa

The volcano at Krakatoa, between Java and Sumatra, erupted 100 years ago this month. It killed 36,000 people and the explosion could be heard nearly 5,000km away. The effects could be seen as far away as Britain!

Smell Survey by Airwick
Top Ten Odious Odours!

1) Smelly feet and socks
2) Stale tobacco
3) Cheap perfume
4) Cooking
5) Pets
6) Rising damp
7) Traffic fumes
8) Wet paint
9) Stale alcohol
10) Wet washing

September

Thursday *September 1*	Roland Rat is going to be replaced by Popeye on TV-AM.
Friday *September 2*	Gale force winds and mountainous seas off the south-west coast. The QE2 drops anchor off the Isle of Wight as small boats shelter from the storm.
Saturday *September 3*	British Long Distance Swimming Association Championship from Lakeside to Waterhead on Lake Windermere, Cumbria.
Sunday *September 4*	Cab Driver of the Year Competition in Battersea Park, London. The gold medal that Daley Thompson won in Helsinki is stolen from a car in Piccadilly, London.
Monday *September 5*	Second anniversary of the setting up of the peace camp at Greenham Common in Berkshire: 21 women are arrested for obstructing workmen laying pipes.
Tuesday *September 6*	Daley Thompson gets his gold medal back (see Sept 4) – it was found in a post box in Trafalgar Square!
Wednesday *September 7*	Queen Elizabeth I was born, 1533, at Greenwich Palace. The river Biss at Trowbridge in Wiltshire is turned into a large bubblebath after shampoo spills into it from a factory. New Moon
Thursday *September 8*	Rescue operation is mounted to save a school of whales stranded in the Blackwater Estuary in Essex.
Friday *September 9*	Rare Breeds Survival Trust's Show and Sale at the Royal Agricultural Showground at Stoneleigh, Warks.
Saturday *September 10*	Thamesday on the river Thames in London. United Kingdom Fireworks Festival in Plymouth.
Sunday *September 11*	A long-nosed Potoroo (female) is born at London Zoo.
Monday *September 12*	Animal Liberation Front releases about 3300 mink from two farms at Brome, Suffolk, and Canewdon, Essex.
Tuesday *September 13*	Lucky, a small brown dog found wandering the streets in the East End of London, becomes the 2,500,000th dog to be taken in by the Battersea Dogs' Home.
Wednesday *September 14*	Mrs Thatcher inaugurates Britain's Magnus oilfield in the North Sea.

Thursday *September 15*	The 137m Old Man of Hoy, the tallest sea stack in Britain, has been bought by the RSPB for £115,000.
Friday *September 16*	Princess Anne opens the National Exhibition of Children's Art in London.
Saturday *September 17*	A rescue operation is launched to save hundreds of rare wild orchids (Autumn Lady's Tresses) threatened by drainage works near Sutton Bridge, Lincolnshire.
Sunday *September 18*	Twenty-five animals are blessed at the annual Pets Service at Alexandra Park United Reformed Church, London.
Monday *September 19*	Start of the Round England Relay Race at Berwick-upon-Tweed, Northumberland, to raise money for British athletes at next year's Olympics.
Tuesday *September 20*	Lucky (No. 2,500,000 at Battersea Dogs' Home) is claimed by his family. His real name is Scamp!
Wednesday *September 21*	One of the dullest Septembers this century.
Thursday *September 22*	Two-hundred-and-twenty-four animals (horses, cattle, sheep, pigs and goats) and 2 vets trot on board a Noah's Ark at Poole, Dorset, bound for the Falkland Islands. Full Moon
Friday *September 23*	A giant windmill on top of Burgar Hill, Orkney, starts producing electricity from wind power with 18m propellers.
Saturday *September 24*	English National Karate Championships at Crystal Palace Sports Centre in London.
Sunday *September 25*	Mass escape from the maximum security Maze prison in Belfast, N. Ireland.
Monday *September 26*	A male Orang Utan called Cain is born at Bristol Zoo.
Tuesday *September 27*	Tony Murray (8), of Barrow-in-Furness, wins his own weight in tea and becomes National Cub Scout Tea-Making Champion after making 2713 cups of tea in a fortnight!
Wednesday *September 28*	The Leaning Tower of Pisa has increased its lean by slightly less than a millimetre over the past year— according to the official survey!

Thursday *September 29*	Dame Mary Donaldson is elected the first woman Lord Mayor of London since the office was established 791 years ago, in 1192.
Friday *September 30*	The 36.5m chimney at Whitbread's Exchange brewery in Sheffield is demolished. The detonator switch is triggered by the toppling of 2000 dominoes, laid out by the world domino-toppling champion, Michael Cairney.

September

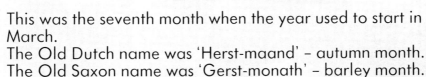

This was the seventh month when the year used to start in March.
The Old Dutch name was 'Herst-maand' – autumn month.
The Old Saxon name was 'Gerst-monath' – barley month.

September Sports and Records Board

Robert McLaughlin ends his circumnavigation of Britain by canoe at County Hall in London on September 4. It took him 143 days to paddle 2093 nautical miles!

Steve O'Shaughnessy scores a century in 35 minutes for Lancashire against Leicestershire at Old Trafford. He equals the world record set by Percy Fender 63 years ago.

Richard Noble, from London, drives his jet car Thrust 2 at a record land speed of 622.637 mph across the Black Rock Desert in Nevada. It doesn't count because it was only a one-way run!

A world speed record for a scheduled passenger train is set by French Railways, covering the 424.8km from Paris to Lyons in two hours at an average speed of 212.4kph.

Australia captures the America's Cup yachting trophy from the USA for the first time in 132 years.

William Neal, from Salcombe, sets out from Helsinki on the final stage of his journey from London to Leningrad in a bath with a 4.5 horsepower outboard engine.

TOWN CRIER 16p	SNOOPER 18p	DAILY BULB 20p	THE GOOD EGG 19p
NOAH'S ARK SETS SAIL FOR THE FALKLAND ISLANDS	PRINCESS ANNE MEETS SAM – THE OFFICIAL MASCOT OF THE LA OLYMPICS IN 1984	INDEPENDENCE FOR ST KITTS AND NEVIS	GOVERNMENT SAYS NO HUNTING OF GREY SEAL PUPS THIS YEAR IN SCOTTISH WATERS

October

Saturday *October 1*	Yiannis Kouris (27) wins the first Spartathlon, from Athens to Sparta in Greece, in 21hrs 53mins 42secs.
Sunday *October 2*	Mike Richardson, a butcher from Ealing, wins the National Sausage Competition in London.
Monday *October 3*	Horse of the Year Show starts at Wembley Arena.
Tuesday *October 4*	Boys' Brigade Centenary Day. The *Mary Rose*, Henry VIII's flagship which sank in the Solent in 1545, and was raised last year, goes on public display in Portsmouth.
Wednesday *October 5*	The Post Office issues four new stamps to mark the 850th anniversary of St Bartholomew's Fair, Smithfield, London. Emma Bufton (13) from Wells, Somerset, becomes Junior Cook of the Year with parsnip and gooseberry soup, Somerset chicken surprise and oatmeal meringue.
Thursday *October 6*	Chay Blyth sails under Tower Bridge in his trimaran, *Beefeater*, on his way to America and an attempt on the Round the Horn Record. New Moon
Friday *October 7*	Happy 106th Birthday to Mrs Clara Blunt, of Willingham, Cambridgeshire! The worst drought for 60 years in South Africa is broken by rain and thunderstorms.
Saturday *October 8*	Roland Rat returns to TV-AM after a brief rest.
Sunday *October 9*	Sandy Rowan (68) beats 63 competitors to win the 19th annual World Conker Championship at Ashton, Northants.
Monday *October 10*	Soviet space probes, launched four months ago, have reached Venus and are in orbit.
Tuesday *October 11*	A single rocket is fired from the roof of the National Theatre in London in tribute to Sir Ralph Richardson, the famous actor, who died yesterday.
Wednesday *October 12*	Halley's Comet, due to pass near Earth in 1986, has been seen by astronomers at a distance of 1,400,000,000 kilometres through the world's largest telescope in the Caucasus Mountains.
Thursday *October 13*	Happy Birthday, Mrs Thatcher! Vegetables and flowers beware a new pest—the American Serpentine Leaf Miner.

October

This was the eighth month in the old Roman calendar when the year started in March. The Old Dutch name was 'Wyn-maand' – wine month. The Old English name was 'Winter-fylleth' – winter full moon.

Halley's Comet

Halley's Comet was first recorded in China, hundreds of years before the birth of Christ! It was observed here in 1628 by the Astronomer Royal, John Flamsteed, and by Edmond Halley, who was the first person to work out that the comet travelled in a huge orbit and not in a straight line. He said that it would return in about 76 years – and it did!

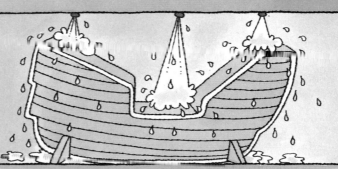

The Mary Rose

The hull of the *Mary Rose* is sprayed with icy water for eighteen hours a day to prevent the timbers from drying out.

Oct. 5: The Post Office issues four new stamps to mark the 850th anniversary of St Bartholomew's Fair in London.

16p 20½p 28p 31p

STOP PRESS!

Richard Noble, from London, breaks the world land speed record in his jet car *Thrust 2* at an average speed of 633.468 mph. This time, it was over the required two runs!

Friday *October 14*	The space shuttle, Columbia, due to carry the European space laboratory into orbit later this month, is delayed by a fault in the starboard rocket nozzle.
Saturday *October 15*	International White Cane Day. Ferries from Ramsgate, Kent, and Douglas, Isle of Man, are cancelled because of severe gales. Trains between Waterloo and Guildford are delayed by fallen trees.
Sunday *October 16*	The Biggest Acorn Hunt in history is launched to find out how many of London's oaks have been attacked by an insect called *Andricus Quercuscalicis*.
Monday *October 17*	Reports in the US warn of global warming and the greenhouse effect. Two Whooper Swans arrive at Welney, Norfolk and 5 reach Martin Mere, Lancashire.
Tuesday *October 18*	Butlin's holiday camps at Clacton, Essex, and Filey, Yorkshire, are to close!
Wednesday *October 19*	The European rocket, Ariane, with a 2-tonne communications satellite on board, is launched from French Guiana.
Thursday *October 20*	Soviet unmanned spacecraft, Progress 18, is launched to carry equipment to cosmonauts living on the orbiting space station, Salyut-7.
Friday *October 21*	The Queen opens the new Burrell Gallery in Glasgow. Full Moon
Saturday *October 22*	The first 3 Bewick's Swans arrive back at the Wildfowl Trust, Slimbridge, Gloucestershire, for the winter. Monocole and Spectacle are seen at 8.30am, and Investiture in the middle of the afternoon.
Sunday *October 23*	British Summer Time ends when the clocks go back one hour at 2am. *Superdogs '83* at Wembley Conference Centre.
Monday *October 24*	Shao-Shao, a nine-year-old panda, mother of Chu-Lin (who got stuck up a tree on April 24), dies at Madrid Zoo.
Tuesday *October 25*	The world's heaviest monarch, King Taufa'ahau Tupou IV of Tonga, lays a wreath on the tomb of the Unknown Soldier in Westminster Abbey.
Wednesday *October 26*	David Clegg (10) from Bassett, Hampshire, becomes Chorister of the Year.

Thursday *October 27*	Two lynx leave a zoo in Derbyshire by helicopter, on the first stage of their journey to France, where they will be released into the wild. Lynx died out there about 100 years ago.
Friday *October 28*	The Noah's Ark that left Poole in Dorset in September arrives in the Falkland Islands.
Saturday *October 29*	Tonight is the coldest October night in central London since records began in 1940!
Sunday *October 30*	A huge earthquake in eastern Turkey kills at least 500 people.
Monday *October 31*	Hallowe'en. Fifty-two Bewick's Swans have arrived back at the Wildfowl Trust at Slimbridge in Gloucestershire for the winter now.

October 16

The Biggest Acorn Hunt in history took place:
Battersea Park
Sydenham Hill
Parliament Hill
Victoria Park
Wimbledon Common

Portrait of an American Serpentine Leaf Miner

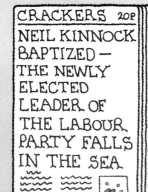

CRACKERS 20p

NEIL KINNOCK BAPTIZED — THE NEWLY ELECTED LEADER OF THE LABOUR PARTY FALLS IN THE SEA

DAILY OAK 18p

LECH WALESA, LEADER OF THE POLISH TRADES UNION SOLIDARITY, IS AWARDED NOBEL PEACE PRIZE

SPOTLIGHT 24p

MASS CND RALLY IN TRAFALGAR SQUARE, LONDON

THE HADDOCK 21p

HOW MUCH FOR YOUR TEDDY BEAR? TOY BEAR SELLS FOR £350 AT SOTHEBY'S

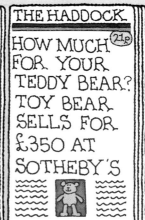

November

Tuesday *November 1*	Two Soviet cosmonauts, who have been in space since June aboard Salyut-7, work outside the space station for nearly 3 hours, fitting an extra solar-powered battery.
Wednesday *November 2*	The Queen unveils a statue of Admiral of the Fleet Earl Mountbatten of Burma on Foreign Office Green, London.
Thursday *November 3*	Daniel Jenkins (13), from Wiltshire, is awarded the Golden Medal and Red Ribbon for services to Austria. He saved an Austrian boy who was on holiday in England from drowning.
Friday *November 4*	Britain's longest locomotive nameplate – CONFEDERATION OF BRITISH INDUSTRY – is unveiled in Glasgow. New Moon
Saturday *November 5*	Games Day at the Royal Horticultural Society Halls in London.
Sunday *November 6*	RAC Veteran Car Run from London to Brighton: a 1903 Mercedes is first to cross the line.
Monday *November 7*	A Viking woollen sock is being prepared for display at the new Viking museum in York. It will be hand washed in purified water, dried and mounted on a wooden foot: cost £800.
Tuesday *November 8*	Eastern Belgium suffers its most severe earthquake since 1938. One woman is killed and several people are injured.
Wednesday *November 9*	The Queen leaves Heathrow airport for State visits to Kenya, Bangladesh and India. The Lord Mayor of London lets her six grandchildren try out the golden coach which is getting ready for Saturday.
Thursday *November 10*	King George II was born in Hanover, Germany, 300 years ago today. Hundreds of children audition for the musical *Oliver!* at the Aldwych Theatre in London.
Friday *November 11*	A large green monster suit, with rubber antennae that appeared in *Dr Who*, is sold at Sotheby's in Chester for £160.
Saturday *November 12*	Lord Mayor's Show in London. Lancelot, a Bewick's Swan, returns to the wildfowl Trust at Slimbridge, Gloucestershire from Siberia for his 21st winter.
Sunday *November 13*	Remembrance Sunday. British Hexagonal Chess Championships in London.

November

This was the ninth month in the Old Roman calendar when the year started in March. The Old Saxon name was 'Wind-monath' – wind month! The Old Dutch name was 'Slaght-maand' – slaughter month!

Bewick's Swans

At the beginning of November about 40 Bewick's Swans are seen each day at the Wildfowl Trust at Slimbridge in Gloucestershire. They are back from their breeding grounds in the Arctic to spend the winter here. The numbers gradually creep up to the first major 'swan-fall' during the week-end of November 12–13. Altogether 281 are counted this winter. They can be identified because each swan has individual markings on its bill, rather like finger-prints! Some birds return year after year, like Lancelot, who has brought with him his third mate, Elaine, and their two children, Excalibur and Pendragon. The swans are named after a famous 18th century ornithologist and engraver, Thomas Bewick, whose telescope is still used at Slimbridge.

November 25: The Five Dr Whos

William Hartnell
Patrick Troughton
Jon Pertwee
Tom Baker
Peter Davison

DAILY WHIZZ 21p
THE SPHINX'S BEARD — BRITISH MUSEUM AGREES TO RETURN BITS TO EGYPT

CHEEP 16p
THE OLD VIC THEATRE RE-OPENS UNDER NEW MANAGEMENT

NEPTUNE 19p
DOWN WITH LONG-LIFE MILK A 6M LONG MILK BOTTLE FLOATS UP THE THAMES IN PROTEST AT THE IMPORT OF CHEAP EEC LONG-LIFE MILK

YODEL ☆ 20p
CRUISE MISSILES ARRIVE AT GREENHAM COMMON IN BERKSHIRE

Monday *November 14*	A chimpanzee, Kan Kan, is born at Chester Zoo to Boris and Kate.
Tuesday *November 15*	John Prescott (45), Shadow Transport Secretary, swims from Chelsea Bridge to Westminster along the river Thames, in protest at the Government's policy of dumping nuclear waste at sea.
Wednesday *November 16*	Princess Alexandra switches on £75,000 worth of Regent Street Christmas lights in London. Heavyweight boxer Frank Bruno gives his 21st birthday cake (in the shape of a boxing glove) to Great Ormond Street Hospital.
Thursday *November 17*	Miss UK wins the Miss World Contest at the Royal Albert Hall in London.
Friday *November 18*	Girl sextuplets are born in Liverpool.
Saturday *November 19*	Start of the Lombard RAC Rally from Bath — 10am. A stretch of beach near Sellafield in Cumbria is closed after radio-active material is washed ashore.
Sunday *November 20*	Lio Jingxian (39) wins China's best cook competition with a menu of fish stomach, bear's paw, sea slug and chicken's legs. Full Moon
Monday *November 21*	The Prince of Wales abseils 24m down a cliff at St Donats in Wales with students from Atlantic College, and then climbs back up!
Tuesday *November 22*	Sarikei, a female Orang Utan, is born to Dennis and Martha at Chester Zoo. An African Brush-tailed Porcupine (male) is born at London Zoo.
Wednesday *November 23*	A new plastic pound note goes into circulation on the Isle of Man. Two Soviet cosmonauts return to earth after nearly 5 months on board Salyut-7, the orbiting space station.
Thursday *November 24*	Princess Margaret pays tribute to twelve Champion Children of the Year at the Savoy Hotel in London, organized by Barnado's.
Friday *November 25*	Dr Who celebrates 20 years on TV with a special adventure called *The Five Doctors*.
Saturday *November 26*	Largest theft in British history: six masked and armed robbers steal 3,000kg of gold, valued at £25,000,000, from a security depot near Heathrow airport.

Sunday *November 27*	Tripper, a black-and-white border collie, is awarded a medal at the Pro-Dog dinner in London for saving the life of his master—twice.
Monday *November 28*	American space shuttle, Columbia, with a 6-man crew, including one West German astronaut, takes off from Cape Canaveral in Florida.
Tuesday *November 29*	The World Wildlife Fund and the Woodland Trust launch a scheme to save Britain's oak trees. 
Wednesday *November 30*	Concorde reaches 2,188.2kph—twice the speed of sound—on the first supersonic scheduled flight from Heathrow to Edinburgh.

Nov.16: The Post Office issues five new Christmas stamps

Champions of 1983

Rose of the Year	Beautiful Britain
Newspaper of the Year	The *Observer*
Miss Pears	Gemma Plant (3)
Miss World	Miss UK (Sarah-Jane Hutt)
Brain of Britain	Gabrielle Malloy (16)
Mastermind	Christopher Hughes
Bus Driver of the Year	Roger Burge
Supreme Champion at Crufts	Montracia Kaskarak Hitarie
Pup of the Year	Belroyd Love Bird
Pipeman of the Year	Patrick Moore
Toy of the Year	Star Wars toys
Supreme Cattle Champion	Cheers
World Conker Champion	Sandy Rowan
British Scrabble Champion	Colin Gumbrell
Time Magazine Award	Ronald Reagan
Man of the Year	Yuri Andropov
Champion Show Jumper	Apollo II (Geoff Glazzard)
Junior Cook of the Year	Emma Bufton
National Cub Scout Tea Making Champion	Tony Murray
Show Business Personality of the Year	Wayne Sleep
Yachtsman of the Year	Richard Broadhead

December

Thursday *December 1*	Cabbage Patch Kids which cost £24.99, including birth certificate and adoption papers, arrive in Britain.
Friday *December 2*	More than 1000 people a day are going to see the *Mary Rose* in Portsmouth now.
Saturday *December 3*	Twenty-four-hour patrols on Christmas trees in the New Forest to stop them being stolen.
Sunday *December 4*	Partial eclipse of the sun, visible from Greenwich from 11.40am to 12.28pm. New Moon
Monday *December 5*	A rare Pied Wheatear is seen in Paignton, Devon, more than 19,000km from its winter home in East Africa.
Tuesday *December 6*	Supreme Champion at the Royal Smithfield Show in London is Cheers, an 18-month-old Charolais-Aberdeen Angus crossbreed, weighing 571.54kg.
Wednesday *December 7*	China has issued a special silver panda coin in honour of International Year of the Panda.
Thursday *December 8*	Space shuttle, Columbia, lands at Edwards Air Force Base in California, after 10 days in space.
Friday *December 9*	Gales and storms. The Christmas tree in Trafalgar Square, London, is almost blown over. Happy 106th Birthday to Miss Louie Hemington of Boston, Lincolnshire!
Saturday *December 10*	The comic *Buster* has carried out a survey which shows that their readers' favourite TVprogramme is *Knight Rider*. Best films are *E.T.* and *Star Wars* and the top dinner fish and chips.
Sunday *December 11*	A memorial is unveiled in Poole, Dorset, to the Cockleshell Heroes of the last world war.
Monday *December 12*	A 25m high King Kong balloon on the front of the Cumberland Hotel in London, celebrates his 50th birthday and the hotel's which is also 50 this year!
Tuesday *December 13*	Father Christmas gives a children's party at 11 Downing Street, London, the home of the Chancellor of the Exchequer, Nigel Lawson.
Wednesday *December 14*	Ten Children of Courage are presented with their awards at Westminster Abbey.

Thursday *December 15*	A suspicious package which Army bomb experts blow up at Castle Green in Bristol turns out to be a jigsaw puzzle!
Friday *December 16*	A Christmas tree is put on the pavement outside 10 Downing Street, London, for the first time.
Saturday *December 17*	A car bomb explodes outside Harrods, killing 5 people and injuring more than 90.
Sunday *December 18*	The first Whooper Swan arrives at the Wildfowl Trust, Slimbridge, Gloucestershire for the winter.
Monday *December 19*	Busiest day for the Post Office! About 250,000 cards postmarked *Reindeerland* are being delivered to children who wrote to Father Christmas.
Tuesday *December 20*	Carol singers from fruit farms in Kent perform at dawn at the New Covent Garden Market in London. Full Moon
Wednesday *December 21*	The wax figure of George Orwell, who wrote a famous book called *1984*, goes on show at Mme Tussaud's in London.
Thursday *December 22*	Shortest day of the year. Sunrise: 8.04am. Sunset: 3.54pm. Snow storms and record low temperatures in the USA.
Friday *December 23*	A 4-month-old Rottweiler puppy, Toby, gets his head stuck in his dog flap in Bournemouth and has to be cut free by firemen!
Saturday *December 24*	William Hill, the book-maker, is offering 50–1 against it being a White Christmas! Cub Scouts from the 15th Long Eaton Pack in Derbyshire have sent a giant Christmas card measuring more than 30m to the crew of *HMS Fearless* in Lebanon.
Sunday *December 25*	Christmas Day swims in front of the Royal Victoria Hotel, Hastings (10am), and on Albion Beach, near Palace Pier, Brighton (11am). 37°C in Sydney, Australia 12°C at the London Weather Centre.
Monday *December 26*	It is so cold in America that oranges freeze on the trees in Florida!
Tuesday *December 27*	Two more Soviet satellites are launched—Cosmos 1516 and Cosmos 1517.
Wednesday *December 28*	Sunil Gavaskar of India makes his 30th Test century against the West Indies at Madras, beating Sir Donald Bradman's record of 29.

Thursday *December 29*	One-hundred-and-twenty skiers are stranded for nearly 12 hours in cable cars near Lugano in Switzerland before they are rescued by helicopter.
Friday *December 30*	Dutch chrysanthemums are banned from Britain for three months after white rust disease is discovered in a shipment from Holland.
Saturday *December 31*	Len Rush, the Queen's racing pigeon manager, retires after 22 years. The fountains in Trafalgar Square are boarded up in preparation for tonight's celebrations!

December

X This used to be the tenth month in the old Roman calendar when the year started in March. **X**

For Sale

LLANFAIRPWLLGWYNGYLLGOGERYCHWYRNDROBWLLLLANTYSILIOGOGOGOCH
Asking Price: £180,000

The Cockleshell Heroes

Forty-one years ago, the Cockleshell Heroes paddled 96.5km in canoes through enemy territory, in a raid on German ships in Bordeaux, France.

Children of Courage 1983

Jerome Kiflingbury (13) from
  Reading
Lorraine Topham (8) from
  Manchester
Sharon Parkhurst (10) from
  Leeds
Shaun Nethercott (12) from
  Exeter
Richard Neale (11) from
  Bearstead, Kent
Carl Dickinson (12) from
  Huddersfield
Angela Carruthers (4) from
  Dumfriesshire
Brenda Marshall (11) from
  Dumfriesshire
Andrew McLean (5) from
  Preston
Sarah Foggon (11) from
  Tyne and Wear

Reindeer!

The only herd of reindeer in Britain live half-wild in Glen More Forest Park near Aviemore in Scotland. There are about 60 of them and their keeper calls them with a special cry that they can hear up to 1.5km away. Nine reindeer calves were born in May!